night in negative

poems by

mischa pearlman

for my parents, alan and britta.

~~CONTENTS~~

there is some order to the poems in this book, but not enough to list them. they were written over a period of years – the oldest ones, i think, i wrote in 2001 and reworked for this book, but most of what's included here was written from around 2010 or so onwards. there's no chronology to this collection, however. dive in at random or read all the way through. these are slices of life - ever fleeting, ever fragile – that take in death and love and loss and friendship and family and heroes and politics and everything that fills the gaps in between or falls outside. i hope you enjoy them.

thank you to anyone who's ever read a word i wrote
or inspired me to write, intentionally or otherwise.

cool blue new

kind of blue on new year's eve
and i'm a william claxton snapshot -
sucking grey smoke from black and white,
inhaling the last 50 years deep into these
uneducated, unborn lungs.
past blakey and baker and billie,
dexter, ella and monk,
right through from bird to the birth of the cool.
my fix is deep blue notes
sung from rooftops
where, underneath, jack kerouac may have smacked benzedrine lips
while ginsberg hummed foreverness.
i am out of place
i am out of time
and out of sync.
miles away and counting
as 1959 becomes one more year ago,
another second in the past,
another minute into time,
always slipping slowly into history,
yet still somehow right here, right now -
and feel those notes, that blow, that sound
those hands, that mouth, those concentrating eyes and skin like night,
sweat dripping off his face like rain
as coltrane waits his turn
and cigarette smoke freezes just off-centre of the frame,
waiting to rise high into the sky to turn to cloud
and then fall back down to earth again, reborn as dust,
once more alive like the deep blue cool of now.

was

wrote a note on my hand,
but accidentally washed it off.
it was an idea for a poem.
it was the first time we met.
it was the curl of your smile when you laughed.
it was the scent of your skin in the morning.
it was the sound of your voice when you cried.
it was the pattern of your breathing late at night.
it was the last time we spoke.
it was the stale air of an airplane cabin.
it was the musty dust of train carriage seats.
it was the nuclear glare of sunlight creeping through the blinds.
it was the smell of summer in the winter.
it was the fear of war and the hatred of fear.
it was the atom bomb blowing up america.
it was a homeless veteran asking for food.
it was the cure for cancer.
it was proof of the existence of god.
it was a plan to change the world.
it was a reminder to pay the gas bill.
it was insomnia at 5.08am.
it was a wish to fall asleep.
it was a hope to stay awake and never stop writing.
it was the absolute meaning of life.
it was a total understanding of death.
it was black lines of biro on my palm,
now smudged, obliterated, faded.
it was nothing at all.

snohomish

the bridge was train tracks
stretched across a river
beyond a fence
we could have climbed
we should have climbed
we didn't climb
that day.
we swore with bitter breath
the next we would.
we never did.
not because
we didn't want to be a cliché
like the movies -
because that *stand by me* nostalgia
makes my bones break still -
but because
we never made it back
and time ran out
like coal and steam and train tracks
that stretch across a river
beyond a fence
behind a tattered sign with peeling paint
that says 'no trespassing'
as waves lap hungrily below
and ghost trains speed across in fury
as decades pass in minutes
and seconds turn to years.
i never even took a fucking photo.

3

we are the sons and daughters of avarice and corporate anaesthesia

with iphones for hearts we stood patiently in line,
playing candy crush saga while we waited for the shots.
we signed our souls away, numbed ourselves and dumbed ourselves,
boxed up our grandparents' dreams with their dead bodies
and forgot, again, about the past.
we woke up five years later, hungry and hungover,
took two aspirin to quell the ache
then checked our emails and our twitters and our facebooks
and realised billy joel was wrong.
the world continues to turn
and we just let it burn,
throwing ourselves into the flames, matches in hand,
because we were the ones who set it alight.

clara

...and suddenly the sadness strikes you,
you walking out of the jazz club
down cobbled copenhagen streets 'round midnight
past a busker busking dylan's *blowin' in the wind.*
and how appropriate, you think, with a funeral in your heart
and others on your mind, that things get blown away
and families slowly disappear.

the hotel minibar is empty - no more comfort
save an inch of vodka rotting warm above the fridge
like one final pre-death breath left hanging in the air -
so you curl above the sheets and listen to the streets below
as one lone lost gravelled voice floats
through the window with the breeze,
a drunk drinking drunker so as not to feel the night.

you imagine his fingers curled red around
a crushed cheap can of beer, holding onto life,
hoping they won't find him like that in the morning,
that he has one more day to drink and forget
although what he drinks to forget
he drank and forgot a long, long time ago.
but then he starts singing - something in danish -

and he almost sounds happy and you forget, too, the day just gone
and the life that went with it.
silent save for CNN, you're born again
in a sterile copenhagen room - a child alone -
waiting for all the wonders of the world
to unfurl themselves once more before
ferlinghetti's smiling mortician
knocks upon the door.

warm and wasted

the heat in london reminds me of our first time in new york -
sticky restless and impossible to sleep.
up early from the jetlag
drenched in sweat and dreams
unpacking bags to create
some permanence in a temporary home.

brooklyn was dry and dusty, warm and wasted,
its streets sad and stained - like two broke-up lovers'
unwashed sheets on a bed unmade for weeks.
we traced the sidewalk cracks and subway tracks
famous trademarks and public parks,
mini-marts and shopping carts
full of rheingold and hershey's, wrigley's and miller,
mountain dew and alka seltzer
and, in amongst the pancake mixes,
aunt jemima's bright white beam,
smiling hard to forgive the past.

windows open, we sweat beneath the covers here and now
pretending to be there and then - or anywhere or when
that we don't have to think or work or try too hard
to just be us and happy.
well-travelled back in time through cans of beer,
we are briefly there through humid air
to smell the hot rain on the street
and sing along to love and alcohol
and thoughts we've loved for years.
but we know all too well
just how the past will pass - come sunrise,
new york will disappear again
replaced by tired, dried, hayfevered, london eyes.

in the end

i was going to take a picture of you sleeping.
you looked so peaceful and content,
far away from the horrors of this fucked up world
and the struggles of our daily lives.
i wanted to show you that things can be okay,
even if it's just in dreams,
that the real nightmares are all outside this room,
that, as the saying goes,
everything will be okay
in the end.
but then i thought better of it -
maybe you wouldn't want to see yourself like that
because then you'd know how and who you weren't
and how and who you could be
and you'd stand before the mirror
holding yourself,
comparing your faces,
and you'd never sleep again,
waiting for the end.
so i kissed you on the forehead,
and then on both your eyelids,
put my phone away,
tiptoed out the room,
shut the door and left for work
again.

silence and strangers

the sun sets in the window of the bus
as we wind our way to california.
my thoughts are with you, ginsberg,
in your supermarket, in your baggage room at greyhound.
this is still your world, fifty years hence,
less buddha, more bullshit.
crushed and cramped in seats too small
writing, reading, listening, watching silence and strangers,
alone on i-5 between mountains and telephone polls,
black trees, weary limbs and the powder-white dust
of the combine harvesters.
so many more hours to go and all of them for you.
we are all in this together.
nothing left to do but wait -
for the sun, for the night, to collect our bags
and to search the slopes of san francisco for your shadow,
for your soul,
for your grimacing, grinning ghost.

almost almost

the last time i was here, you were still with smiles and eyes.
and all i can think of, speeding through these country miles,
is your grimace death skull deep beneath the ground,
alone and waiting without thoughts or love.
i wandered through the same old streets,
drank cheap bad coffee in the same old haunts,
passed on your news to those you knew.

they say hello. they say goodbye.

and passing our old house as dusk approached
i tossed a stone up at your window
to try to break the stillness in my heart.
all i got was broken glass and angry screams.
so i ran drunk fast into the lamplit afternoon,
remembering much younger feet on these same streets,
back when we had smiles and dreams,
and i almost almost laughed.

this is a long drive for someone with everything to think about

back before taxes and the end of the world
we drank and drove for nine days straight
and turned to gods in a valhalla of our minds
as we cruised down highways full of tourists every starless night.
but we made sure the photographs we took were empty and serene -
a paradise lost, with cars and people out of sight.
because it was just you and me, my love,
and there was no such thing as time,
just telegraph poles and trees,
rain and roads ("egyptian ruins, our first kiss" my head sang)
and a blockbuster video, still open,
somewhere on a highway in wasilla, alaska,
its blue and yellow sign
glowing lonely in a sky not dark enough to care.

not yet written

i dreamed of allen ginsberg last night.
he was in a whorehouse somewhere in america,
wondering what to do
with the vast array of T&A
that was on display in front of him.
and i was right there too,
fourteen years old
and long past childhood
with bruises and lipstick and bright blue mascara
and judy garland cheeks.
i saw him, bearded and balded,
trying not to listen
to the southern accents arguing
through marlboro breath
and absinthe teeth
but looking at me with those smiling, small, sad eyes
full of befuddlement and buddha
and he stepped towards me and held out his hand
somewhere in a whorehouse in america
and i led him gently to my room and closed the door.
his hands were soft and his beard was soft and it smelled like tobacco
and he held me in his arms and he couldn't understand when i told him
that this was the safest place for me to be, here among the old and
haggard whores who reeked of perfume and sloppy sex and all the old
men who passed through and paid me well and sometimes extra and who
didn't ever hurt me all that much, and then allen ginsberg held me even
tighter and we smoked a joint together and he read me a poem he'd not
yet written and we laughed at the clouds that formed inside the rose red
room and everything suddenly made sense.
but then i was gone
and he was still there,
in a whorehouse somewhere in america,
lost
lost
lost.

i'm afraid there's nothing more that we can do

alcohol breath
counting steps,
tinnitus leaking
from your ears
like life from limbs
crushed beneath wheels
- "did you hear? they say
he'll never walk again."

old photographs,
unwritten books -
the slow tick
of the clock.
dead skin
turns to dust
and ghosts glide
through your dreams.

firehouse

peewee left the firehouse.
no more rum to soothe his nerves,
wipe out his mind,
to cleanse his dirty fingernails.
there was a picture of the 151 (so-called)
placed atop the sage's grave, both cindered,
its ashes mixed with his,
flames reduced to flames by flames.

peewee drowned his sorrows in the fire,
caught alight and then caught flight,
scattered by the wind across the town.
in nighttime silence you still can
catch his pearls of wisdom
dripping from the stars,
a wise man's words whispered by the wind:
"wash off the blood, wash off the 151."

flurried

place bets that it'll snow on christmas
and i'll bet that you'll be wrong.
better with no expectations,
no childhood fantasies reborn
of virgin crystals landing on your tongue.
yet still you'll try to lie upon the ground
like all those years ago.
but a fallen angel's flapping wings
seem heavier than ever now,
so much more desperate, dark and tragic
these years on.
and you remember running with
the dog and with your parents
through the endless fields of white
behind your house
and falling down
and throwing snowballs
and catching colds
and snowflakes on your tongue
and shivering at seventeen,
naked, cold and crouched in tears,
no central heating,
watching through your window
as the world you knew began to change again
for good again
flake by flake by flake.
like melting snowmen -
petrified, immobile -
we last until we can,
hold fast until we can no longer
and we slowly slip away
into the ground beneath
to be held there captive
for the rising morning sun.

low-lit (for DH)

late one valentine's night
i read your emails for the first time in years -
no longer digital but printed and dog-eared
and full of a younger man's older hopes.
though we both remain who we were then -
captured on paper, preserved in ink -
who we were then we can never be again.
i still see you sometimes
when our continents collide,
maybe once every two years
and i remember and remind you of your words,
enthralled at how our worlds diverged
and how i'd hoped they could always stay the same
in my dumb, naive, romantic way.
yes, i still see you sometimes,
but it's never long enough
to recapture what was lost - the last time
on a wet and windy norwich afternoon
just minutes before i had to catch my train
(my past derailed once again)
to pass through my old homes -
but it's enough to share the smiles
of all the miles i never thought we'd gain
from all the things i never thought would change
but that i knew deep down could never stay the same.
so late one valentine's night
in an ever romantic daze
i read your emails for the first time in years,
your words, low-lit, lying loosely on my desk,
our traumas waiting to unfold.

bloodless

the room is edward hopper,
dusty sunbeams shedding light
across the unmade bed.
i pin myself against the
shadow crucifix
created by the window frame
but there is no stigmata,
only the gentle cushion of the pillows
and the tousled, slept-in sheets.
across the road,
the bright white church stands
tuesday quiet
as i lie in patient, painted nostalgia.
armageddon, i am waiting.

long-haul

deep within these bones, that airport kind of loneliness -
the lacuna of leaving but never arriving,
perpetual farewells
dulled by free booze and dimmed lights.
long-haul flights every night
in a cabin full of stagnant air and strangers -
scraped out from the inside
and forever fleeing from the future,
ghosts gliding through metal detectors,
lost in the limbo of time zones,
of dead and empty space.
loose change, left luggage.
strong coffee, weak resolve.
layover hangover
and the empty weight of everywhere
you always were but never are.
"say hello, and it's goodbye again"
but you can't remember which came first.
there's just that airport kind of loneliness
as days pass by like nights
that always turn to day too soon.

regressive tendencies

sneaking out of the lecture hall,
feeling like we're 15 again
with too little to lose
to not choose
to laugh and run through the cold air
towards a bus
that takes us
to the first signs of christmas;
roasted chestnuts, skins included,
and toy stores
that conjure up a past
so near in time
so distant in mind
and so perfect as present
that we feel 10 again and decide
that 8 would be a good age to be
again,
if only for today.
but maybe
you and me,
together,
now,
like this,
without our inhibitions,
would be just a little bit too perfect.

not even god can save us now, america

numb drunk on a new york summer's night
we had conversations with computers
auto-tuned for the perfect customer response,
each phrase smiled from beyond bad jazz
while we sweated out frustrations,
head pounding with tomorrow's hangover.

sloppy drunk watching late night television
we muted all the ads and then turned the damn thing off
but still the corporations shouted,
stole our voices and our votes
while we sucked up the cost through ice pop teeth
and con ed charged us by the second for our comfort.

happy drunk in the almost dark, the night and years marched on
to the sound of sirens racing in the street
to save a life or maybe take a life
while we hid like kids beneath the covers,
lost to memories of youth and dreams of peace,
with neither within reach.

slumped

with tongues scorched black with wine and all that brings
we talked about the things we loved back then
before we left to start again.
you were slumped against the sofa,
so far gone you could barely see,
your spine pressed back into my knees.
we plotted our escapes without a thought they might come true,
that we would one day reach beyond the shadows,
and i played you *point blank*, some live version on a bootleg full of the
madness and the sadness of the end of the world and we sat there in
silence and listened to it, hoping for it,
shot between the eyes,
unaware the years were passing by already,
the continents dividing, drifting slow like snow,
bloodless brothers trapped in time and decades still not lived or lost.
and we raised a can to distance and dreams
and a reality realised with the sobriety of morning and its fond farewells,
the futility of the future at our fingertips.

atrophy (for JW)

you lie in green silence,
a paused VHS -
still but still flickering.
your skin
like snowflakes
ever
so
gently
falling down,
graceful
and cold,
to melt back into the world.
i hope that you are dreaming,
not just dying.

earthquakes and airstrikes

it's always dusk outside the kitchen window,
a heavy hue of blue or grey or something in-between
that just hangs stagnant;
a silence waiting to be broken.

we ignore the news as best we can,
not from indifference or apathy,
but because our hearts weigh heavy
with the exhaustion of just trying to get by

in a world rife with inhumanity and injustice and racism and war and
ignorance and political corruption and corporate greed and earthquakes
and airstrikes and daytime TV and wall street's recklessness and police
brutality and for-profit prisons and the propaganda of mainstream media
and mass inequality and wealth disparity and sports stars and celebrities
and the dumbing down of culture and the rise of trump and the
stronghold of the oligarchy and the status quo and american 'freedom'
and the military-industrial complex and how the pursuit of happiness has
become a quest for wealth and fame and how, really, when it all comes
down to it, we're all just fucked.

sometimes, i forget there's life beyond these walls,
that there's more outside than just that timeless vacuum
and the occasional pigeon attempting to make a home inside it
before i scare him off.

so we cook and eat, do the dishes, read out loud, play records,
pretend there's nothing else to do,
that there's no need to worry,
that we have all the time in the world,
even as
the world
burns down
around
us.

chekhov

i miss the space where you paced
and then sat and guarded me in white.
with sad brown eyes you talked to me,
uttered words i could never understand.
i still spoke back.
but i don't think you knew i said goodbye.
or rather, i don't think you knew i meant goodbye.
so i returned one dumb, drunk night
expecting you
expecting me
and there you weren't,
save static traces clinging to the rug
like tiny ghosts stretched thin around the world.
i couldn't even call to leave a message.
so now i type your name in code each day,
but seven years for each of mine
takes far too long to fade away.

never enough

and time runs out as always,
fast or slow,
slips away like childhood dreams.
we sit alone together,
so many years silent,
so many smiles apart,
so many words thought
there is, was, always wish that there will be
the touch
of fingertips coarse
on skin as smooth as tears.
everything shared and everything lost
left with ghosts
who scream in darkness
during dreams and nightmares -
quiet nights
ups and downs
alcohol breath
burning hearts and bleeding lips
red eyed absolution
forgiveness and regret
scare away the memories.
one last moment together
is never enough
and so we clutch at air
and space to keep us there.
like childhood dreams
we slip away,
fast or slow,
and time runs out as always.

insomniache

fell asleep in the afternoon and woke up so much younger,
grey sky dazed in an english autumn with the radiator clicking into winter.
you had sunk into the bottom bunk,
your childhood toys with chew marks scattered at your feet,
each bite clockstopped, tick-tocked, unforgotten.
but then the jolt, the rush, the roar of parents calling you to dinner,
you shouting back and stomping down the stairs,
feet heavy with excitement.

awake on a train in london rain
you start to miss these grey cloud skies
as the national return you to your childhood
even though they weren't there for it.
your mind becomes your room,
the bed messy and unmade
as it often still is now and you wonder where you've been
and where you're going and where you know you'll never go.

early mornings turn to 3pm too quickly
and inspired nights just turn to tired nights -
wordless and worthless and wasted and wounded,
waits howling out that it ain't what the moon did
but you can't even see the moon from where you're slouched,
passed out at last and fully clothed, eyes black and red and grey.
don't pretend that you're awake.
you've not slept properly for years.

night in negative

there are some nights - apocalyptic, holocaust winter-cold summer nights
full of wind and stabbing static rain as i'm walking towards the bus stop
with my fingers frozen curved arthritic around a half dead can of beer -
when i want to call you, just to hear you smile. i always never manage.
instead, i walk along with the same songs in my ears i had ten years ago,
with the same feelings in my veins, alcohol as love as blood, and i take my
voice as yours, invent your words to answer mine. and even on the bus,
slouched back against that rubber bending with every turn of phrase and
road, i move my lips to speak words i wish i wrote and said as the wind
battles harsh against the windows, and the air fights itself with the smell
of cold and over-fried chicken every time the doors slide open and
particles collide.

and on those nights the journey spins as my mind fills with words
unspoken phrases unmade reminding me not to drink and think at the
same time ever never ever again. sometimes, sleepy drunk, i'll miss my
stop, end up months away or years ago and when that happens, craving
cigarettes to be desperate, romantic, hungry, alive, awake like blake
(schwarzenbach not william), i'll walk the extra minutes through those
months and years on cracked grey pavements and wish i was someone i
admired so that this weathered smile would be worthwhile, if only for the
few nervous-heart seconds it exists. and then in that dying, darting rain,
exhausted tired drunk again with thoughts of work and the evils of a
pretty face, i finish that stale crushed can, if i've not already dropped it,
and try not to stumble home.

and in my unmade double bed at last, beneath my cold open window
sheets i heartbeat fast and close my eyes and feel like i'm watching my
mother cry, holding her to me, trying to console what can never be
consoled, saddened by the trembling tears i hoped i never had to see or
wipe or talk away.

and and and and all it takes is one short phone call, a few short words,
some shaken woken memory brought to life through wires and buttons,
the imagined structure of your mouth, curved, curling, caring, cutting, to

make reality unreal, to feel what isn't felt, to dream what once came true.
and on those nights i shake and shudder judder like the bus journey home
and finally – "about time!" say tired limbs - let decades turn to eyelashes
and collapse alone into the darkness of an alcohol-lined mind until i wake
to shake once more to breathe and rise again and try to remember how
and where and why and who and when the fuck you ever weren't.

expired

i sit and read *kaddish* with death on my mind,
the angels of old age raging while i drink
to find some solace in your absence.
there is none.

the apartment hums with the buzz of electricity
giving life to light and light to life.
the fridge shudders to occasional attention.
i'm hungry but i'm not.

the jazz on the radio is perfect for this sunday gloom,
as daytime chases night and summer turns to fall once more.
i start to read again the beginning of the end of life;
that morbid comfort of fake immortality:

"strange now to think of you," i say aloud in allen's voice,
"gone without corsets and eyes." but these are my words now
and greenwich village is a world away, across the river on the L
and my pass expired yesterday and i am tired anyway -

tired and not yet drunk on wine,
the neighbors kids' playing in the hallway,
the cat asleep beside me on the sofa, oblivious,
my black sweater covered in her hair,
coltrane blowing on his sax as darkness falls outside.

...like a river that don't know where it's flowing

it was drunk and i was dark,
brainwashed and rainwashed
and stuck in the past
on a cracked east london street,
beside myself and seeing double,
stumbling on sodden feet
as a storm came crashing down
as a night bus rushed right by
as a couple kissed against the wall
beneath the bridge ahead,
a headache coming on
but each swig sweet relief
as tattered shoes smacked battered ground
swerving but unswerved
nervous but unnerved
just following the footsteps
of springsteen's *hungry heart*
and its fatalistic future
step by step by step
by step by...

pledge of allegiance

the red, white and blue turned black again,
as decades steamrolled back again—
dr king turned in his grave
and then was shot and killed once more,
bleeding out from too much too
while the government just laughed.
and JFK today remains long-dead,
head snapped back and to the right,
buried with the truth in arlington, virginia
as history repeats
and building seven freefalls every day.
in babylon's broken playground
the neo-libs and neo-cons shake hands and laugh
while the flag flies behind them at half-mast.
its stars become black holes,
its stripes run crimson red
but money's being made -
it doesn't matter if we're dead.

bad sleep on good dreams

your silhouette smoked a cigarette in the corner of my eye last night.
i couldn't see your face, just its distant orange glow
as i passed by below, huddled with a headache
and heading straight for home, to try to sleep for want of dreams.
i couldn't see your face, but i imagined that i knew you,
that we'd shared some distant past,
some fleeting look or drunken night or wasted years
we only half-remembered in the morning aftermath.
the bitter, biting cold broke all my brittle bones,
neck strings snapping as i strained to catch a glimpse
of the future missed or decades lost
you exhaled into the air.
too high to be rebreathed, reclaimed, returned,
or to even know i know you, though i know i know i don't,
your silhouette a cigarette dissolved into the night.
i couldn't see your face - will never know your face -
but heard the words you whispered as i tried to fall asleep.
never knows best, you said. never knows best.

a good place to come and die

outside the flamingo bar on a winter afternoon
jack sucks a cigarette and stares at the grey st petersburg sky,
his eyes alive and wide and full of the folly and the fury of his future past.
"how the hell did i die here?" he asks himself,
as happy hour offers 3 drinks for 5 bucks
to the sad eyed fucks who sit there drunk at 2pm
and remember being promising
before the wonder of their youth
ruptured like their livers,
became as sallow as their skin.
frozen forever before that final drink,
jack kicks back in black and white -
almost smiling, almost smiling -
as a sad grey rain begins to fall in florida
and his body slowly starts to fill with blood.

in the deep heart of the night

the low glow of your phone in the mirror
turns us into spectres for a second or two
before our reflections fade back
into another too-short night.
our eyes adjust and everything we need
flickers static black
just out of reach.
through the open window
i hear the rain hit the warm city streets
and a distant bassline pumping
with the promise of an unconsidered future,
the reckless infinity of youth.
and you are asleep before i even have the chance to say goodnight,
you, lying in the dark like an angel on my chest -
and i hear those words run through my mind as i think them,
remembering first times and missed signs
and the damage we avoided and the hollows still to come
as faces of friends lost and gone flash through my mind
one by one by one by one by one
like it's fucking dating app,
yet still i close my eyes to see more clearly.
and you're still still, still tucked inside my arm
when a car alarm goes off outside, insistent and ignored
until it turns to shouts and screams and sirens -
then scattered shots - then silence for a second
before another hell breaks loose...
and all i do is close the window.
full of memories and fear,
i put my arms around you.
"one day, my love," i whisper, "we're going to disappear."
but you don't hear, just barely stir and move your feet
while i lie there and listen to the space between my heartbeats.
when the morning light arrives,
casting sun across our bed
you wake me with a kiss and ask me how i slept.

as empty as

on a dusty typewriter
devoid of ribbon,
lacking in black,
i type to write
but fail,
as much on paper as in mind.
nothing more to say, perhaps,
or just no other way to say it.
see, we went through all the motions
all the trials and tribulations
of late night/early morning phone calls
and an eternity of desperation -
pleading
crying
begging
faking
swearing
lying
hating
shouting
gently gently gently sobbing
into lonely palms no longer held by yours.
yet still, as centuries have passed
and generations died,
no change -
just left with nothing more
than daytime television,
memories and wine.
and so as red and white denial breeds
red and white desire to
read and write words
that never will be seen,
on a rusty typewriter
devoid of ribbon
yet never so black

i type to write
but fail,
my words as empty
as a starless winter sky
about to rain.

the ghost forests of alaska

the earth cracked and broke
like teenage hearts in 1964,
died screaming.
swallowed towns like they were lives,
crushed lives like swatting flies,
chewed metal and bone like gum -
centuries and memories torn down
in the length of a pop song -
4 minutes 38 - but there never was a chorus.
and now the land is littered
with trees as grey as cancer
and as weak as your last gasp,
ghost forests constantly dying
but never quite dead,
a broken clock that doesn't even tell
the right time twice a day.

carpe diem

i want to be america.
i want to live american.
don't know why
because tonight the stars shone bright
and this place felt like home
and even more.
yet still something longs.
thoughts of ginsberg, kerouac, springsteen, schwarzenbach.
open-road hitchhiking beneath a sky like now,
as ferlinghetti's frail, fragile home draws me into the future,
calls me from a past i never knew.
and i want my life
now and then
here and there
this and that -
all of it all at once.
dreaming my friends everywhere.
can only meet so many people.
i recollect the east coast/west coast blur of diction
making truths out of my fictions
and i want, too, to speak and shout like that,
to breathe the early morning air
and live the early morning hours
in intensity burnout,
sucking in the mist while europe wakes.
my curtain hides the stars
but still they taunt me.
i need to do more than just exist.

hurricane grey

the hangover lasts all day,
as long as the rain in montauk
and its sheets of hurricane grey
that bring apocalyptic end of summer scenes -
deserted beaches, near-empty hotels
and the isolated farmhouses
that the train ploughs past,
where time stands still inside
as weather whips their windows,
and the cold creeps in
beneath our skin.
back in the city, we lock ourselves away,
pop alka-seltzer like skittles,
watch the wind torment the trees
as sirens sing red, white and blue
in some otherworldly distance
that we pretend to not notice
from inside our yellow glow.
and the temperature drops
and the rain comes down
and the lightning strikes twice
and memories flood the street,
bouncing off the tarmac
and washing into storm drains
where, dirty grey and destitute,
they bubble with intent,
a hangover lasting for years.

ice-cream headaches

give me chet baker, cigarettes
and a bottle of blood red wine.
give me restless nights too warm to sleep
and big gulp ice-cream headaches.
give me calvin and hobbes summers,
the way you always knew it could be.
give me mosquito bites and hot rain
and dreams that still itch.
give me shel silverstein lines,
board games and superheroes.
give me drunken midweek mornings
passed out on your sofa.
give me daytime naps and mixtapes
in a pre-internet age.
give me your lips the first time we kissed
and your eyes just after the last.
there is no correlation.
give me morning sickness and alcohol sweats,
hair of the dog and camomile tea,
old friends and funerals,
dead cups of coffee
and a sink full of stained washing up.
give me greasy spoon breakfasts
you're too weak to eat.
give me that first sip of tea
and a brief hug goodbye,
the sun stretching itself out across your face
as you walk through the quiet, lazy streets,
knowing there will never be a next time.

california dreaming (for carl sandburg)

the night is fog in san francisco
and it glides like sandburg's metaphor
across the lights of the evening city.

one day, i want to tiptoe
like those cat feet
across the bay.

one day, i want to be
as regular
as fading daylight.

one day,
for just one day,
i want to be here forever.

still

new york, you lie behind the curtains, taunting me,
but i am still in love with you, even if my pockets are empty
and my dreams are tired and it's 1.38 in the morning and i am in bed
wide-eye exhausted, having done nothing i'd planned to do today or even
this week or maybe for the last five years.

but that's okay, because you are the city of dreams -
especially in winter late at night like nights tonight
when there's nothing to do
and nowhere to go
and no-one to see
(*why isn't the heating on? it's too damn cold in here!*) -
even if those dreams feel like they cost too much and everyone is tired if
inspired from just trying to make rent and not live like animals, which was
never part of the deal now, was it?

but still i lie here, still,
still behind these curtains, the lights of the brownstones across the street
mostly all out now because it's after 2am and everyone's asleep like i
should be but my mind is busy whirring churning crunching,
frank o'hara by my bed, the lonesome crowding west inside my head,
and i'm trying to decide if i should write my thoughts and live or simply
close my eyes and dream.

pompeiied

last night i met -
i spoke to -
listened to -
wide-eyed, drop jawed -
a girl who moved to NYC
on september 10, 2001.
and i watched her eyes fill
as she remembered skies fall,
death clouds swimming
down the avenues
on her first full day,
her brand new world
crashing down
collapsing
creaking
like a broken branch
hanging in the wind,
time draped dali-like
across the city's ruins.

but then, september 12, 2001 -
because life went on
because life goes on
because life won't stop
when we become bones -
and she is subwayed,
stuck beneath the empire state,
cops and tourists running
in dumb blind panic
as a bomb scare spreads like wildfire
through 34th st station.
outside at last, she runs
past telegraph poles
completely covered
with missing people.

she knew, she said,
that everyone was dead.

not stopping to think
or thinking to stop
she charges below 14th street,
into a dense, dark, stagnant cloud
of death and dust
and she's on her knees
retching
crying
puking up
a thick black tar
that chokes her as it leaves her throat
in thick heavy clumps that stain her teeth
and as she coughs she worries
that she'll never stand back up
but be freeze framed forever,
pompeiied inside the centre of the storm
a day after the world already stopped.

as she spoke i could see her
count the days
and count the years
and count the faces
from the posters that she says
she still remembers
running by that afternoon,
september 12, 2001,
not just as if she knew them
but as if she knew them well,
as if they were her friends
as if they all were still alive
and as if, each year,
she has them round for wine
and they raise a glass
to toast her moving here.

independence day

july 4, sometime near midnight, some year now gone,
we lay down in the cold dark air
to remind ourselves what stars were.
i could feel the wooden deck, still slightly damp from the afternoon's rain,
on my skin through my clothes,
the silhouette of spruces forming a frame around the sky.
and it was maybe the wine that was thinking
but as we waited there for fireworks or thunder
all i could imagine was some rotting, flesh-dead hand
rising from the jet black water
and tearing us apart.
there was only the tranquility of fireflies,
silent neon pulses in the air
flickering like first cigarettes.
you were trying to read me something
but your eyes wouldn't work at night
and the words stayed on the page,
waiting to be brought to life.
we, too, wanted to not just be alive but feel alive
and tried to fall asleep outside together
arms stretched around each other,
the vast night watching us like
we were characters in a film.
but there wasn't enough wine
to soothe the frigid air
so we gave up,
went inside,
turned on the TV
to forget about the night outside
and we sat there, silent, holding hands,
imagining all the possibilities.

another empty bus at shit o'clock

ride through london backwards
and it's a city out of sight and out of time.
strangers sneeze and eyeballs dry
as doors shut open - *shut up! fuck off! fuck you!* - and open shut
and headaches start the hangover as men shout silently outside,
never seen, never unheard again.
and the piss in my gut is painful
but i've learned to keep it in
like all those thoughts reduced to silent smiles.
i can't even see the sky, can barely feel the miles,
just apathy and exhaustion on a tuesday morning
that had just been monday night.
moving backwards to go forwards yet again.
moving forwards to head back once more.

almost almost

the last time i was here, you were still with smiles and eyes.
and all I can think of, speeding through these country miles,
is your grimace death skull deep beneath the ground,
alone and waiting without thoughts or love.
i wandered through the same old streets,
drank cheap bad coffee in the same old haunts,
passed on your news to those you knew.
they say hello. they say goodbye.

and passing our old house as dusk approached
i tossed a stone up at your window
to try to break the stillness in my heart.
all i got was broken glass and angry screams.
so i ran drunk fast into the lamplit afternoon,
remembering much younger feet on these same streets,
back when we had smiles and dreams,
and i almost almost laughed.

hollow isolation

just off the george parks highway,
this is what could have been, what could be still -
a snow white shell left unfulfilled, unfilled,
its never-opened doors now boarded,
broken, left to melt in hollow isolation.
20 miles from cantwell (population 222)
its abandoned beams, cracked windows, bare cabins
all break with slow decline,
decaying in denali desert snow.
on the outside, graffiti marks naive romance,
"i ♥ you this big" sprayed in scrappy, heartfelt handwriting,
the sentiment abandoned but alive,
much like the rotting couch discarded
by the weeds now sprouting in the driveway.
and where the gas station never was
the fuel pumps are missing
and empty beds and rooms that never were still aren't.
sometimes, the curious pull in,
and truckers tired from their long distance trails,
but mostly there is just the silence of the mountains
and the sound of what could be,
what could have been,
what never was
and what will never be.

ARP

the world ends every day
but they still play jazz
in washington square park,
and it reminds me of you
and of childhood -
warm winter evenings in canterbury
with chess sets and fires,
wondering where the wild things are
and who miles davis is
and why the world is sad and mad
and hearing you speak
the words of the beats
and teaching, always teaching,
all i needed to know.

past perfect

a broken walkman offers no relief
from this disease, caught from a stolen kiss
in cathedral grounds
one warm, october summer afternoon.
and as autumn trees move past my window
i am travelling again
and living out a dream that can never be achieved;
my perfect past, recreated.
fuzzy sound and garbled words cannot stop
my thoughts from turning
to the lines down my cheeks
that you once wiped away.
and as this tongue now tastes
the bitterness of canteen food
instead of your soft kisses
i miss that sunny afternoon.
you said to always travel, always smile,
so on a train, going somewhere,
i smile to no-one
and think of you.

permanent hibernation

winter got you, turned your red blood blue, dampened down your nerves. you walked white through white streets, risen like an undead christ, slouched and slumped and never looking further than your feet. it was just in case you slipped or tripped, you told yourself.

time froze like the rain on the streets, and just like the snow it wouldn't melt, condensed instead into a reminder of the months you couldn't shake, the pills you didn't take, the work you wouldn't do, the food you didn't eat, the lies you tried to fake.

and the alcohol burned your throat like cigarettes, stuck like a cancer that couldn't be cut out, beer cans collecting at your bedside. beyond the blind, the world outside - mornings turned to morning with nothing in between. somewhere, childhood memories were forming in the snow.

bloodshot, you lost yourself inside yourself, each day the same, each day the same, each day the same, each day the same. stone cold and silent, you didn't even notice when the season broke to resurrect you, the springtime sunshine thawing out your bones, its warm light resting on your skin.

and there is still some snow in the yard of the house down the block that used to be one but is now split into bedsits, divided into fractions, waiting for you to walk past one last time, emerged from permanent hibernation to gaze upon its majestic roof, its windows slightly open, the smell of summer almost in the air.

(un)familiar

so weird to see you now,
how - now - you balance your mouth
like a waitress with a tray of drinks
about to fall and spill them all
and maybe break a glass or two and
cut a jagged line across her skin.

but you, you keep your blood in
and your heart and teeth polite,
not quite the person i remember in those photos.
rather, an imposter in a stoic, brittle shell -
cracked slightly on the inside -
of the you i knew so well.

tunnel vision

all i can think about, 3.52am and waiting for the subway, is your
body on the tracks. i'm not sure if it's before the train hits or
after death strikes, but i see you lying down there, little more
than flesh on bone, electricity pulsating, the taste of too much
whiskey in my throat, sore feet restless for deep sleep.

too tired for heroics, i watch the rats surround you, feel the
delay through your decay years later, rats gnawing at grey flesh
and brittle bone. but then, in front of dirty tiles and approaching
lights, counting squares like stars to stave off these subterranean
nightmares, a wayward smile of absolution.

there is no time down here. just you and i, my dear, and all our
drunken fears. but i realise i could live among the rats with
tunnel vision, breathe underneath new york, feral and alive and
always chasing, running between boroughs, never in service, never
getting home to wherever home might be.

and even if i knew that i could halt the crash and save your life - soothe
your charred and pungent flesh, haul you up, reverse your death -
i don't know if i would. and so, for now, i wait bone drunk for this train
to end tonight in the hope tomorrow always comes,
watching rats scatter before the blast of cold plastic air,
their lifeless eyes black and impenetrable, starved and starving.

broken suitcase

vast blue and vivid green
fill my dreams of then
back when we were one long dusty highway.
we sliced through texas and its morning roadside breakfasts
glimmering with grease and our greatest expectations
as wheels spun past polaroid snapshots of vacant car lots
and bankrupt bail bond offices offering freedom for a fee,
where the slumbered homeless slept through the afternoons,
too drunk or weak or dead
to wake just yet.

and in these restless visions, sweat clings to clothes
and weathered veins bulge blue through tanning skin
and fingers twine tight as white knuckle drives
take us far from our origins to render us lost
cross country in that crisis-ridden continent
searching for a future
that was outlined by the poets of our past
and which we kid ourselves is hidden somewhere
in the desert's brimming, burning, ever-setting sun.

from greyhound station to greyhound station,
decade to decade, state to state,
the same sad hand grips a broken suitcase
and writes postcards never sent
because they can never be delivered,
like dead roads traced on crumpled maps
that can no longer be traversed,
that only exist on paper now,
inches long and miles short
of the vast blue and vivid green
that fill my dreams of then.

america is gone

perhaps it's your perfume that reminds me of new york
but london smells like america tonight -
candy flossed and codeine scented.
the pizzeria's late night orders
float through the window and the rain,
wine stained and garlicky,
as another summer sets.
there is no autumn, just the fall
and a sad face full of smiles.
through the wall, next door's television
blares muffled lives into our limbs entwined
and beneath the sheets the coffee on your breath is death -
raw morning nerves and cigarettes,
the sticky, sickly, salt-sweet sweat
of missing love and hard times debt,
a life of work and fading dreams
like dirty shirts that always go unironed.
and though i swear i thought i smelled you twice today
i know i'm wrong. that's just a song -
america is gone and the new york streets are far too far away.

once, these shoes were new

marks and scars increase with years,
each dent a sign of our decline.
the formula is simple -
each step we take
one less we'll make -
but we forge on regardless,
unable to escape
a fate we once never considered.

so now we count in years ago,
in what was done and what was lost,
not what we'll do
and what there is to come.
there are fewer names to put to faces,
old friends not quite remembered -
fractioned and fragmented -
or forgotten altogether.

we, too, are echoes now -
shadows of our shadows,
dead and ruined shoes
scraped and scratched
by the paths we took
and those we didn't -
but we will walk
as long as we can walk,
until the road runs out.

disconnected

on the phone, i always wait the extra second that it takes
for you to hang up first, because i like the rustling
of your fingers in my ear as you slowly switch me off.
i like to think my voice stays with you in your darkness,
wrapped up beneath your duvet as you close your eyes to sleep.
and i always break my promise, which means i always lie to you,
because i always stay up later
and watch the candle flicker tired in the fireplace.
sometimes you catch me listening and i imagine us laughing,
together, flesh, not through wires and plastic.
and then the game is on to hang on forever
(well, for as long as we can manage),
like it's the last breath we'll take
and the last time we'll speak and the last time we'll hear.
you didn't catch me tonight
but i wondered just the same.

infinite murmur

above its piers, three tiers of traffic
tear through brooklyn heights
where elevated eyes stretch towards
manhattan's wounded skyline.
it stares back defiant.
beneath the sunstruck promenade
the rush of trucks and cars
- a driven drone of restless lives,
all engine noise and toxic fumes -
is an exhausting sea of calm,
an infinite endless murmur.
across the water,
vertical ghosts shimmer blue and white.
impossible, then, to now not think
of tumbling towers
crumbling to dust,
rising and reaching
and clouding this picturesque platform
with dark grey smoke and distant sirens
and the putrid stench of burning flesh
and apocalyptic death.
so take my hand, my love, and let us sit
and wait and wait and wait
and watch the world burn down.

my valentine, you're poison now

cold, tired bones from open windows
give us headaches like the winter.
red wine stained and blood drained
on a sunday afternoon,
we pop paracetamol and aspirin
or whatever comes to hand
(all non-brand because it's cheaper
and we can't afford the names)
and count down the next four hours
as our teeth begin to ache.

the floor is stella-littered,
stale warmth in slightly dented cans.
and tonight could be our last night,
so we remember to each other
faces we'd forgotten and girls we thought we loved
to songs we fell asleep to so many years ago.
outside, alive, the sky dims like a slowly dying light
as we close our eyes to thoughts of staplers and spreadsheets
and the crazed and hazy line between what went wrong and right.

cavities of greed

the muzak in the dentist's office offers sweet relief
from the shrill drills in the distance where they fill
lacunae with the gold that should be propping up the dollar.
but these crisp green bills
are no longer what they were, now just
cavities of greed and scraped out suffering,
excavated without morphine,
all bleeding gums and damaged nerves
and blackened, brittle teeth that cannot bite
without breaking or chew without splintering,
shards of enamel slicing as we swallow,
us spitting and shitting until our organs rupture
and we so slowly and so softly bleed out,
full in the knowledge that we're already dead inside,
that there is no choice to this suicide
and even though we know bill hicks was right
when he said that this is just a ride - "it's just a ride! it's just a ride!"-
we watch ourselves get fucked again
and watch our throats get cut again
and watch our mouths disintegrate and rot
and all we do is sit and smile with gap-toothed jaws
and hum along to *yesterday* anaesthetised,
willfully ignoring our decay
until our teeth get yanked and thrown away.

piece by piece

if you could bury your bones,
do you know where you would put them?
because i still smell your scent
and will try to dig them up.
with muddy paws and broken claws
i'd drag you through the earth
until you surfaced piece by piece,
never let you rest.
i would lay you out
in the comfort of a home you'll never know,
peel off your skin
and lick you clean,
gnaw at your cartilage
then suck your marrow dry,
nibble at your eye sockets
crack your skull and break your ribs,
feast upon your spine.
swallow all your teeth
and chomp and chew and crunch
until you splinter into shards -
smaller smaller smaller -
one by one, piece by piece.
i'd never let you sleep.

i'm sorry for the ghost i made you be

at 3am, a stillness, despite these restless legs.
the room creaks like old and brittle bones,
tired from walking for decades.
i am dry lips and shallow breaths,
a heartbeat louder than rush hour.
i feel your breath on the back of my neck,
your fingertips gripping my flesh,
but there is only space beside me,
the pillow dented hollow,
the duvet ruffled empty.
the heat becomes cold,
the cool air too hot.
the thermostat clicks.
the window lightens.
my gut aches, throat swallows.
next to me, my phone -
its LED flashing with a message unread,
its impending alarm waiting to be ignored.
and it's not because of you that i can't sleep
and it's not because of wars waged or old age
or cancer scares or death or a disbelief in god
but just so i can be a leonard cohen song -
"i haven't said a word since you've been gone" -
for however long i can
before dawn comes to break
the sad magic of the night.

those of those

all and far too often
i see the faces of all of those i love
in those of those i don't.
and i can't run away
or hide behind what's left behind
those bitter eyes that memorised
the memories that stretch beyond
whatever we've become
way back into our past.
the last time that i see you
is something i don't need to think about
or fathom just quite yet.
"would that you could touch this angel
in a clutch of snakes," sings blake
to make me smile so sadly once again.
and i guess it's time to leave
because your clutch just doesn't seem
to matter much
or count for more than
wishful thinking anymore.
so close the fridge at 3am,
a tin of curried herring in your hand
and wait for dreams to fuck you up once more.

last exit from brooklyn

get through the night by dreaming
of fucking you
over (and over again).
5am sky and a cigarette ride
across the brooklyn bridge -
the bright lights of this big city
soaked up, sucked in by morning
and now slowed down
through decaffeinated eyes.
a million other lives drive by
as green signs point towards dead presidents
and unspoken, reluctant farewells.

inside-out

these blue skies and your green eyes
conceal the cold that waits outside and
deep within your shallow skin.
your breath is stained with coffee,
sugar sweet and bitter pilled,
your heart spilled from your throat,
your morning mind a mess of memories
and half-forgotten dreams - or are they?
the wind outside is war
and we're its limbless casualties,
bandaged, bloody stumps hiding out for winter,
when we're rarely asleep before 2am
and barely awake by 11, even on the weekdays,
our eyes opening slowly like our mouths every time they yawn
and we are slow and old beyond our age
but we try our best and we're still trying.
so let's get drunk alone and never leave the house
and watch the daylight fade from inside-out.

flash flood

the rain in the headlights looks like snow,
sheets of television interference wrapping shoulders,
hugging strangers in this black and white night.
you cower in the evening alleyways
of sunday shadows and plastic bags,
waiting for morning to take both away
while cars and buses drive past fast to somewhere else.
there is piss in cracked corners and litter in the street,
wet cigarettes and chicken bones and left flesh
drenched like drowned kittens in the downpour
as the dirt of the night
rushes to the drains
and gathers in your fingers, lingers in your drunken heart -
it will never wash away, despite the storm
and promises of stoicism.
your feet, encased in damp,
will never seem so close to the world,
your hands never further from your heart -
yet both ache through with cold.
still you march home, hungry,
past silhouettes swathed in too-bright light,
the kebab store's neon sign
humming lullabies as night and day swap shifts.

super big gulp

around the corner and a few blocks down
past the homeless guy wiping sweat from his brow
and holding out a palm upturned to say
"some change could make a change"
is the 7-11 - open 24-7 -
with its bright lights and short aisles
and chicken wings and chocolate and candy
and medicines and alcohol
and chewing gum and toiletries
and everything you'd ever need
whenever you would need it -
where i buy a super big gulp cup
for $1.69 - $1.84 including tax -
and fill it full of root beer and ice
and snap the lid on tight
and sip through a straw
that true taste of america
before i walk out the door
to once more ignore
the outstretched palm
that needs so much
but bleeds so little
shaking please
as i weave through neon streets
and wipe sweat from my brow
before walking in and then up
to slouch upon the couch
and turn on the TV
and wonder -
as i channel surf and settle
on a kung-fu flick that stars bruce lee
and guzzle root beer thirstily -
what the fuck is wrong with me
and when did i become so cruel?

travelling without moving

this could be england -
grey and green
for miles
like the M25,
the sky a vacuum of colour,
these wheels churning,
speeding to the middle of nowhere
past trucks stopped at truck stops
and smoke stacks
and traffic lights
and crumbling farms
and service stations
and rows of empty trees silhouetted against a winter sky
and the occasional breakdown,
kids strapped into the back seat
screaming,
unable to understand that
they're not going anywhere
anytime soon or ever.

eclipsed

faint red, like ribena over-watered,
we watch a washed-out moon at midnight
and shiver in the february garden.
our generations, reunited once again,
are immersed in bitter air
beneath the pinprick stars.
we gaze upon the spectacle of shadow
as my socks soak up the patio cold.
winter inches gently up my spine.
your liver sucks up the whiskey in your hand.

out here, in country silence stillness,
i am scared of death - or, more precisely, yours,
your impending mortality closer each time
i see my face in the grey hair of your beard
or feel your warm, coarse hand in mine.
so i hug you tight and smile goodnight
with all the strength my eyes can muster dry,
then i leave you in the garden
to watch and toast alone a bleeding moon
fade slowly back to white.

something like real

you burnt the ridges on the roof of your mouth
with a too-hot piece of pizza. "better than
burning bridges," you say to nobody who's here
because nobody is near but you want me to hear
the pun of the pain of your palate from a distance
measured out in farenheit and flesh.
and there's skin hanging off behind your teeth
and it hurts to press your tongue against its home -
however gently - but you do because it makes you feel
something like real,
like that stinging sore
is you alive and living in the moment
now and always, carpe diem, breathing fast
 - breatheinbreatheoutbreatheinbreatheout -
then gathering saliva in your mouth
that taste of aluminium adrenalin
which you spit red into the sink
to slowly dilute pink and swirl away
unseen but not forgotten
before the septic clean of listerine
swills around your gums and you begin
to count to 30 slowly like your teachers taught you
gargling with pain and patience
and with no more thoughts of pepperoni
even though your gut is empty
even though your head is old
even though your heart is drunk
because you're just not hungry anymore.

hallmark holiday

sick to the stomach with memories and alcohol,
confusion and illusions of what we ever were,
i wake on a cold and rainy february afternoon
to find you're still not here.
sleeping with my arms around the cruellest dream,
i hold you tight and pull you close
and whisper the same sweet nothings
you spoke when you were mine.

remember how we hated valentine's,
ignored each year its plastic love and shopfront sentiments
in an act of romantic defiance?
we took arms against the masses that day,
slaughtered corporations and their manufactured feelings
because we didn't need or want their words -
those we didn't speak on bedroom afternoons
were always more than enough.

funny how we never celebrated valentine's
when we were us
but now that we're just you and me
i want to buy you all the ways to say "i love you"
that my wallet will allow,
just to hear you tell me one more time
that you still do.

imprecise wonder

through this lens the night is blurred
and there are pixels where the stars should be -
infinity condensed and smudged
by technology's myopic eye.
there, beyond the ill-defined darkness,
lie planets and galaxies
uncaptured and uncharted,
solar systems snapped with imprecise wonder
to be uploaded as instant nostalgia.
but i recall the real reality of old,
lying with my arms out in a daze -
"staring at the stars through an ocean haze" -
and joining the dots of all the gods
that hid behind them then
and hide behind them now.
are you, too, still there that new year's eve
when we were in your parents' garden
with empty beers
and a bottle of wine
and much older hearts
than our teenage minds?
the wonders of the skies,
stretched out tight around us,
seemed well within our grasp.
little did we know,
when held inside our palms,
we'd render them redundant.

hell above earth

the curve of the earth is covered with clouds
and as the plane glides slowly above them
i imagine everything below them
coming to an armageddon end
and we're doomed just to fly until the fuel runs out
because there's nowhere left to land
among the fire and the flames,
the famines and the floods,
the fighting and the fury.
so we keep going till the engines sputter
but it's hell above earth here too
because everyone is terrified,
not so much of dying
but knowing that they're dying soon
and there's nothing they can do except panic or pray
and neither does a goddamn thing.
so i just close my eyes,
turn up the volume on my ipod
and try to enjoy the ride.

about to choke (for vic chesnutt)

stupid preoccupations with your pronunciations
find me about to choke some ten years on.
wheelchair-bound, your strange translations
turned to soaring skies and unseen satellites -
new transmissions of the same old let downs,
the sad clowns and broken crowns
are rhymes of times gone by.
drowned in silver lakes by your slowly shutting eyes,
you let the pills do their work.
you didn't realise
they meant you no harm.
i'll see you around
in your new town.

watermelon kisses

waltzing on the rooftop with watermelon kisses,
this is new york, night-time,
moonlight, sky-high,
wide-eyed smile excitement.
drunken hearts and parting lips
give way to now, to here, to this -
to ice-cold beer on an airless night
as we float among these brooklyn lights
and its endless, dirty, dusty, desperate streets.

we live only for the night and would die for it as well,
or so we tell ourselves,
immersed head-first
in jazz and taxis,
sirens, horns and subways
and in the relentless summer hum
that sings softly, slowly, sweetly
and will soothe us
and will cool us into sleep.

you are still as we spin; the world revolves around you
in a blur of sound and light -
blue red white and green and new york's other shades of night.
time ceases to exist
except in promises and kisses,
all made, all stolen in the dark.
and with imaginary strings
beneath imaginary stars
we pretend to fly the kites
we say we'll fly in central park
when tonight becomes tomorrow -
if we decide to ever let tomorrow steal tonight.

peanut butter bagels

we didn't get to see your bones grow
nor hear your marrow stretch.
hidden deep beneath flesh,
somewhere far below the sinews of your heart
there was a stillness
that would stop you in your tracks.
rotten from the inside out,
your smile was solely superficial
but you had no idea - how were we to know?
and so you never saw your eyesight fail
or heard your hearing fade
or smelled your nostrils close
or felt your skin dry up
or watched your teeth fall out
while eating peanut butter bagels.
who am i to say
you aren't the lucky one?

the electric storms of early summer

the sky flickers like a broken TV screen,
the calm before the storm.
this is america's goodbye after everything we've seen,
electricity and water.
jet black tarmac memories and midnight railroad journeys
are washed away by rain
but sea salt eyes and the smell of last night's coffee
remind us where we've been,
the endless roads and tired tracks
leading back into the past.
awake in bed at 4am in a bare-wall motel room,
our suitcases neatly packed, we're distracted by the news.
behind the dirty curtains, the window rattles loudly,
interrupting CNN.
we flick the switch and turn it off,
watch the static fade away.

water tower towns

gliding like a ghost through america
you squint through the trees and the early morning sun,
past quiet sunday backyard lives in water tower towns
where there's no poverty or war,
just the grace of god in the gentle breeze
and the promise and the smell of summer.
but then, further down the tracks,
the projects and the problems
and a special kind of hell
for those who can't afford it -
where once there were homes
there are now just houses,
shuttered silent and graffitied,
left to rot like flesh untouched for centuries.
the seat beside me is vacant,
lonely like lips never kissed
as, once more, the scenery shifts,
making it easier to forget the forgotten.
lonely and alone, i remember your joke
about a cup of coffee.
would have been a nice idea.
more to this than drinking fucking starbucks.

solipsism

whiskey sour
morning sickness
means a brittle skull of curiosity.

(she's not been in this deep before)

an active mind
spites tired bones
for a lifetime of insomnia.

(the bed feels emptier than ever)

cold sweats
from old regrets
are her solipsistic nightmare.

(rain reminds her there's a world outside)

sometimes, there's a difference between lonely and alone.

(but only sometimes)

weather damaged

danced in the rain
like the old days
before the war destroyed our smiles.
the thunder crashed like thunder -
louder than guns or bombs -
and lightning flashed
and cracked the clouds,
split apart the streets
like they were trees.
and i thought the world
would fall on me
as i walked home
alone and free
and drenched in warm, dead rain,
both younger and wiser than before
and finally aware,
with a scream and a smile and a laugh
as loud as war,
that we'd been caught
in the storm all along.

boxed

old photographs
frame lives and memories
faded and forgotten.
i hold you in my hands
as you hold me in yours
for what must have been
the last time.
i remember your hat,
stupid and green,
how it made me laugh
as you sang *happy birthday*
tone deaf but pitch perfect.
i feel your skin beneath my thumb
and smell your musky scent
through these dusty pictures -
like you,
unseen and boxed for years.
but each grainy moment a rebirth,
each blurry smile an electric jolt
to a mind of underexposed recollection.
once again developed
and reminded what was lost
i remember just how much i miss
what once was there
when you were.

it always gets early after it's late

thunk too much,
drunk too little -
sunday insomnia, 3.19am.
sleepless legs. restless eyes.
the air conditioner
whirring like your mind.
tom waits sings lullabies,
bourbon-drenched blue valentines,
but even then, it seems, no dreams -
just the vastness of the night outside
where past and present both collide
in distant stars
as uncertain futures beckon,
unready and unwound.

foreign policy

my bus doesn't stop at yours anymore,
much less 82nd street,
which, even an ocean away, feels so much closer than it should.
and maybe that explains my foreign policy
because after all this attrition it's time to withdraw.
i know i know more than those cunts in charge -
with their false promises and insidious smiles, their lies about austerity -
yet still they have the guts to say they care.

impatient at the red light i scratch your name
into my arm as police police the car crash up ahead
and i trace this fake tattoo with fingertips
stained from last weekend's cigarettes -
the come up from the comedown
shuddered by the judder of the bus
as it rolls past the past.
it's may and i'm cold and i want to go home.

bloody mary mornings

the page won't turn itself
but you can't turn it either,
holed up in a hotel
in the city where you lived once.
you drank yourself to death last night
and tried to talk to god
but you don't know what was said.
there's just the trace of a half-remembered smile
from a half-forgotten life.
but those bloody mary mornings
when you slow-danced with the world
on sunday-quiet streets -
you'll never get those back.
and 3 o'clock is morning
and 3 o'clock is night
and 3 o'clock is always on your mind
but 3 o'clock will never be again.
beyond the window,
the city is silent.
you lie awake
and listen to the years pass by.

yesterday's news

our loss was
circumstantial,
situational -
discarded papers
at the station, all
crumpled up
and muddied
by commuters'
dirty footprints.
it was as if
we missed
the 8.06
into st pancras
two days in a row
and our boss just
let us go without a warning.
but really, we'd
misread the signs,
instead aligned
that caffeine-stained malaise
from all those days
stuck behind desks
in london grey
as life and truth
when, in truth, that life
was sucked like smoke
from smiling eyes
to make us unnotice
how lucky we'd been
and how fast our past
had unravelled unseen.
and so, instead, we
merely stood silent -
the living dying dead -
burning our lips on too-large sips

of too-hot, shit-brown coffee,
wishing for more milk, more sugar
and a fuckload more sleep
while we read yesterday's news
and waited for apologies and trains.

combined

we spent the night unpacking books from boxes, just to feel at home.
we sipped wine and tested out the heating and the hi-fi,
cursed the lack of wi-fi,
drank more wine and then some more and then some more again.
excited by bare walls, we forgot to eat, dancing instead on floorboards
we hoped would hold the weight of combined lives
and hopes and dreams and all those books and records, too.
i forgot that night whose books were whose,
which were presents and from whom,
and which i'd owned before i'd known you, before you'd owned me,
their histories erased by time and wine.
and i wondered if we'd ever read them all, all these millions of words
lined up along those shelves inside our brand new living room in excited,
drunken disarray and waiting to be held like long-lost lovers,
each tale hoping to be read
then spread beyond its pages
like the lives imagined in our minds.
and then, like that, the future happened,
pushed aside just like our sheets that next hungover day,
an unconscious morning motion of unintentional intent
that left so much left unread.

dear you

and we ate all the late night pizza that our teeth could swallow
and we watched all the late night shows that our eyes allowed
and we drank all the bottles that our wallets could afford
(which wasn't very much back then)
and we held tight when everything so right seemed so far away.
and we ate noodles in the evening
(and the morning and for lunch)
and we watched the same shows twice a day
and we laughed about the same jokes which really weren't that funny
and we stayed up later just to prove a mooted, muted point.
and we never thought to say goodbye
and we never thought to stay in touch because we always would be
and we never needed words to say just how we felt
and we never made the plans we'd planned to make
and we never took the steps they wanted us to take
and we always smiled and never growled
and we always argued, never shouted,
and we always danced to stupid songs
and we always slept in late and woke up later
and we always locked the front back door before the morning rose.
and we rarely tidied up
and we barely caught the sunrise
and we rarely took the rubbish out
and we never ever cleaned the kitchen floor.
but tonight i'm drinking bleach
and sucking tongues
and feeling young despite my age
and remembering the times when we were here together
and we ate all the late night pizza that our yellow teeth could swallow
with no thoughts of tomorrow or the next day or the last.

resurrection

more of his blood is outside than in, but the boy is alive. stiff, crimson bandages hide holes in his hands and feet. his skin is translucent white. he whimpers slightly as paramedics wheel his stretcher through the hospital.

"fucking kids," says one to the ER doctor. "they were 'playing' crucifixion. friends get three nails in before he lets himself scream. parents rush out, find him pinned to a tree. he's 12."

the doctor shakes his head. "jesus christ," he mutters, without realising. eight minutes later, he does. "this one," he sighs over the ECG's flatline beep, "isn't coming back."

hiroshima

burned into my memory
like the shadows of hiroshima,
you are my fallout
nuclear mushroom cloud.

we hid for years alone together
in our shelter six feet down,
all candlelit dinners
and tin can romanticism.

we waited for the world to end above us,
for the radiation dust to settle
so we could crawl out with the cockroaches
and live as king and queen.

but claustrophobic and impatient
we gave in far too soon,
stepping into the bright
white light of hell above:

nothing more than atoms
we fall apart one final time
disintegrate to dust
and disappear.

enough is enough

walk up the subway stairs to a blast of sea salt sewage air -
that rotten, rotting scent of august in new york,
except it's not summer anymore
and donald trump is on the cover of forbes
and also in the white house
and motherfucker is it cold
and all you want to do is sleep for years - or at least a day -
but that's easier said than done
when you're scared for the world
and you miss all your friends
and you can't help but wonder
if it's all about to end
even though you know you're being crazy
just by thinking that.
there's a dollar in your pocket
and you hand it to a homeless guy who's walking past
because he needs it more than you.
your teeth ache and your heart is warm but worn
and the medication's wearing off
and you can feel your bones beneath your skin.
you smile as he says "thank you"
knowing that the worst is yet to come,
wishing there was more that you could do.

mutatis mutandis

your death is just as sad in any language,
however beautiful it sounds.
and the more things change
the more i wish they'd stayed the same.

there are still no flowers left
to buy to say goodbye
because the more things change
the more they stay the same.

at night, tom waits sings you to sleep
in the cold, cold ground
and the more things change
the more i wish that they would change

because the more things change
the more they stay the same
and your death is just the same in any language,
however beautiful it sounds.

america, scattered

a past hung on walls
stares at you as you sleep away the day,
as you wash away with alcohol
as you burn away with cigarettes
as you float away like ash and angels,
dust to dust.

we drove for years that summer,
slept in cars and drank the rain,
touched sunburnt arms together
living for the wheels and trains
that took us countless miles
from photograph to photograph.

there are pictures of us in brooklyn
and there are diary entries from seattle
and there are cinema stubs from pittsburgh
and there are souvenirs from san francisco
and there are cashout vouchers from las vegas
and there are phone numbers from chicago
and there are greyhound tickets from portland
and there are voodoo dolls from new orleans
and there are tattered magazines we bought at airports
and there are postcards with greetings from asbury park, NJ
and there are secret notes we wrote each other
that we swapped in darkness at 3am on a cramped bus
in the middle of an unseen highway as we passed through
towns we'd never see or know,
hands like twine as we tried to sleep amidst the snores
of other passengers and the engine's roar beneath our tired, sweaty feet.

we lived from room to room
out of heavy bags we dragged
from coast to coast.
we watched TV on broken sets,

made love on unmade hostel beds,
imagined homes in all the cities
we would have to leave behind.

do you remember how you cried in san francisco
on the day i had to leave?
you never looked so sad,
never so beautiful.
you tried to change my mind, to make me stay,
to choose the choice i couldn't make,
but you had to let me go
and summer had to end.

and now we *are* america -
memories that defy chronology,
moments of colour and time
hung on walls
and left, alone, to fade.
we stare back at ourselves
so many years and miles apart,
snapshot reminders of who and what and where and why
we used to be.

hypnopompic

slumped inside an early morning taxi
i hold your hand as night transitions into day.
too early to talk, too late to sleep
we just stay quiet, listening to the rain upon the roof
as new york starts to wake.
i need caffeine in my veins
to feel the hunger in my gut.
the radio plays low
but i don't want to hear the news
the ads, the songs -
i can't relate to that right now.
ahead, a sea of red stretches out beyond the windshield
as another storm rolls in.
i don't know where we're going
but we could be stuck for years,
inching slowly forwards,
rotting with each other peacefully,
the way that it should be.
but then: the sound of sirens,
the red-blue swirl of catastrophe and calamity
against the dismal grey of rain.
my eyes pried open, our hands apart,
your ghost, faint, peers through the window.
i wonder where - and who - you are.

Printed in Great Britain
by Amazon